ACTION THROUGH WISDOM

(BASED ON BHAGAVAD GITA CHAPTER-4)

DR. JAGADEESH PILLAI

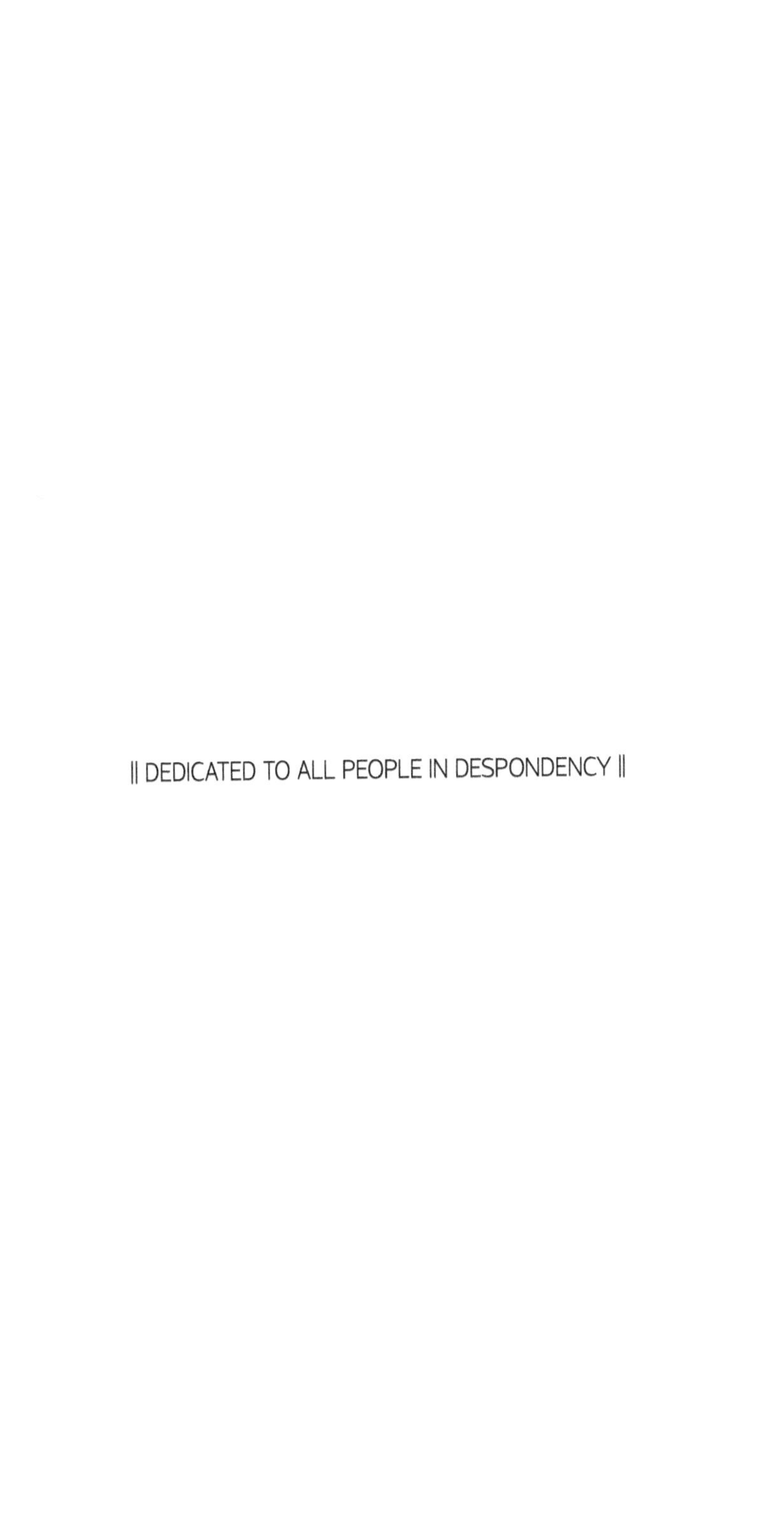
|| DEDICATED TO ALL PEOPLE IN DESPONDENCY ||

Contents

Prayer

śāntākāraṁ bhujagaśayanaṁ padmanābhaṁ sureśaṁ

viśvādhāraṁ gaganasadr̥śaṁ meghavarṇaṁ śubhāṅgam I

lakṣmīkāntaṁ kamalanayanaṁ yogibhirdhyānagamyaṁ

vande viṣṇuṁ bhavabhayaharaṁ sarvalokaikanātham II

About The Author

Dr. Jagadeesh Pillai a voracious reader, Four Times Guinness World Record holder, writer, and true research scholar was born in Varanasi, the abode of Lord Shiva. He is Ph.D. in Vedic Science. He is a multi-faceted polymath with innate qualities, creative ideas and many remarkable achievements. Although his roots extend back to "Gods own Country"(Kerala), the residents of Varanasi feel proud of him and adore him as a child of Varanasi who caters to every individual in need without any expectations. A deep study into his profile reflects that he has added so many feathers to his cap which makes him quite unique. He is a four times Guinness Book of World Records Holder in the following subjects :

"Script to Screen" which he achieved by producing and directing a state of art animation film within the shortest time possible by breaking the earlier set record by Canadians. There are many national and international Awards and Recognitions to his credit.

Longest Line of Post Cards which he has done on the occasion of 163 years of Indian Postal Day by 16300 post cards. The event was also connected with a questionnaire about Indian Flag.

Largest Poster Awareness Campaign – This was achieved by designing an awareness campaign on the subject "Beti Bachao – Beti Padhao".

Largest Envelop – Towards tribute to Prime Minister's initiative 'Make in India' – he has created about 4000 sq meter envelop using waste papers.

Attempted by lighting 70000 candles on a 210 kg cake to celebrate the 70th Indian Independence day recorded in World Records India.

Attempted a documentary on Dhamek Stupa of Sarnath dubbing in 17 languages, result is waiting from Guinness World Records.

He is versatile in Gita teaching. The young generation is fond of his Gita teaching and he has changed the life of many young through his continued motivational boost up and teachings.

He has composed and sung Gayatri Mantra in 1000 different tunes.

He has composed and sung Hanuman Chalisa in 108 different tunes.

He has composed and sung hundreds of Sanskrit Bhajans, Patriotic songs, etc.

He has written and directed so many short films and documentaries for awareness campaigns.

He has done voluntary services to UP Police and Kerala Police to spread awareness campaigns on the various issue through videos and photography.

He is on the path of authoring thousands of books on Indian culture, Indian Temples, and the life of extraordinary people.

It is hard to believe that he has produced and directed more than 100 Documentaries on a particular city (Varanasi) which is done by a single person.

He has helped and guided more than 25 boys and girls to achieve world records through various creative and innovative methods.

A multifaceted person who can apply the best of his intellect using the God-given blessings which have been showered upon every human being granting them an immense capacity to learn, experience, and experiment with many things and do wonders in this world of discrimination and disparities.

He is a teacher and a student at the same time who always learns every day and teaches every day. As a master, his weakness was that he never sticks to a particular subject. Perhaps this weakness gives him the strength to master any area which he came across.

Each of his days dawned with learning a new topic and he spend most of his time experimenting and researching it.

He is also a selfless social activist and a motivational speaker.

His life was full of struggle, ups and downs, and failures. But he never gave up and faced all his trials and tribulations full of confidence. Today he is a successful young man with a lot of enthusiasm and rich life experience.

He has sung full Ram Charita Manas 51 hours audio by his own composition. He has also sung the whole Bhagavad-Gita in his own composition with a rhythmic background.

He has also sung "Lokah Samastha Sukhino Bhavantu" in 50 different languages.

Currently working on a detailed and scientific study on Veda, Upanishad, Puranas, Bhagavad Gita, etc.

Currently, he is the Hon' Chancellor of 'Eurasia Digital University'.

Awards

Four Times Guinness World Records

Winner of Mahatma Gandhi Vishwa Shanti Puraskar

Mahatma Gandhi Global Peace Ambassador
Kashi Ratna Award

Dr. APJ Abdul Kalam Motivational Person of the Year 2017

Mother Teresa Award

Indira Gandhi Priyadarshini Award

Bharat Vikas Ratna Award

Udyog Ratna Award

Vigyan Prasar Award

Poorvanchal Ratn Samman

Preface

The wisdom to practice selfless action (karma), is already existed in the universe since the time of Sun. But we humans are unknown to it.

We never think about the Sun and many such other creatures in nature. Sun is also a part and particle of Supreme like we humans. Sun performs its duty selflessly by spreading light and distributing its energy to every creature, without expecting anything in return. Sun has already achieved wisdom.

Trees also perform their duties and action selflessly. It gives oxygen, fruits, shadow, vitamins, etc. without expecting anything in return.

This book explains how to perform selfless duties and action for the benefit of others.

Dr. Jagadeesh Pillai
PhD in Vedic Science
Four Times Guinness World Record Holder
Winner of MahatmaGandhi Global Peace Award
Author of Many Books

ACTION THROUGH WISDOM

The wisdom to practice selfless action (karma), is already existed in the universe since the time of Sun. But we humans are unknown to it.

For example, the world is not started the day I born, it has existed here before my birth and the actions and duties by its creatures were going on and my birth as a human is also the result of that.

As I have grown up, I forgot the real selfless duties and actions to be performed because of my influence and attachment with physical and material things.

But we never think about the Sun and many such other creatures in nature. Sun is also a part and particle of Supreme like we humans. Sun performs its duty selflessly by spreading light and distributing its energy to every creature, without expecting anything in return. Sun has already achieved wisdom.

Trees also perform their duties and action selflessly. It gives oxygen, fruits, shadow, vitamins, etc. without expecting anything in return.

There are many other creatures' animals, birds like Sun and Tree who perform their duties and action selflessly for the benefit of others only.

But we humans forgot and lost the wisdom of selfless action.

Remember the ancient "Gurukul" education system existed in India, it was extremely different than earlier. The education system these days are mostly concentrated to obtain higher degrees either to obtain a highly paid job or to establish a business. Whatever it is, the main aim is to make more money, accumulate properties and to enjoy luxuries. The value-based education system is no more available. Everyone is running after material things and luxuries.

In the value-based education system, how to get a higher job, how can one make more money, etc. are not taught. But teaches the value of every creature, the value of human, value of soul within you, value of selfless karma towards obligatory duty, value of character, nature, attitude and the value of Supreme (Krishna), creator of everything.

As the generations have gone by, we lost all those good systems of education.

Money and many material things are necessary for the existence of our life, but an extreme desire to earn and collect more and more and later spend on luxuries, etc. are not good.

See...every creature is needed food and shelter, not just humans. Even birds and animals too. If an animal won't get food for a few days, it will die. Somewhere in nature, they will find out their shelter. Some needed and some are not worried about it. But all creatures including human gets up in the morning, passing their days, sleep at night and again continue their life.

But human today is more greedy for everything forgetting some facts of life.

Our days on earth is limited

1. If we have a healthy life of approx. 70 years – 25550 days.

(maximum less than 100 days, if we are unhealthy, no use)

If we deduct our childhood days and the 8 hours' time, we sleep – then we have approx. 10,000 days in a conscious state to perform our duties here.

2. The food we can consume is limited – maximum 2 to 3 kg per

day i.e. 60 to 70 tons the whole life.

3. Even if we have 100 houses or 100 hotels with 1000s of beads around the world, you can occupy only six feet space to sleep anywhere in the world. You cannot choose to sleep in one place every day, the location may change as your moves. It is also not possible that you sleep in 100 beads together at one time. *(Let's recall those days when the world affected with the epidemic of COVID-19).*

4. Last century this day, we were not here (1920), and next

century this day (2120), we won't be here. Whoever or

whatever we are, we have no control over the happenings
of

birth and death.

5. In my perspective, the creature has given no value to your relationships, false desires, bondage and attachments with any physical and material things.

Whomever you love in person, like your son, spouse, friends and whatever material things (properties, etc.) you accumulate, within no time, without any advance information, will be taken back or destroyed.

One of the spouses of newly married couple unexpectedly dies. A young man, his body looks healthy and perfect, suddenly collapse by cardiac arrest. A newly established business started by investing a lot of capital and by taking a huge loan collapses. A lot of luxuries, but you never got a chance to enjoy even 10% of it. You may be happy, that our generation will use it, but that is also unpredictable. Whereat, what stage, what would happen nobody knows.

More

An important quote to note:

People have a false belief that the world started the day they born, because of them it moves, and it will end the day they die. But the fact is, it had existed before you were born and it will be existing after you die. The world will be there, but you won't be there.

Remember the epidemic COVID-19

March 2020 - a small virus (COVID-19), which we could not see by our open eyes, has disturbed the whole world. Every person and family was affected.

No money, power, politics, terrorists, richness, advanced technologies, relations, and attachments – nothing worked out and it has any value.

Countries have invested trillions to make Atom Bombs condenses trillions of atoms in it, to collapse a country or the whole world in war.

But an invisible smallest atom as a virus (COVID-19), has shown the world that thousands of atom bombs are nothing in front of it. It can collapse thousands of atom bombs and the whole world within no time. None of your weapons, technologies, money, power, and politics can do anything.

***

From the above, we understood that we following many valueless things in life. But we never realized and tried to understand it from the other creatures like Sun, trees, etc., the importance of selfless action towards obligatory duty.

In the Gurukul education system, the scholars used to teach us the universal knowledge, tried to develop our intelligence level, and taught culture, attitude, kindness and our duties and obligations towards nature.

The scholars used to take the intelligent test of his disciple assigning them a task complete using their intelligence.

But we lost such a kind of education system in India anymore.

Through one more example, we can try to understand how we lost ancient wisdom and understanding :

Grandfather had a business of selling wooden chairs. There were many other shops of the same products, but the grandfather's shop was very famous and most of the people used to purchase from there, though the prices were a little higher than in other shops.

The secret wisdom behind it was a marketing technique.

Grandfather offered a gift, free repair guarantee and has also gained goodwill by his friendly attitude.

The secret of wisdom behind the grandfather's success through the below example :

1. The retail price of one chair was Rs. 500 (at the wholesale price he got at Rs. 300), then Rs. 200 is the profit margin. Other stores selling the same chair at Rs. 450, but still, most of the people purchase from

grandfather's store only.

2. Grandfather offers (5% discount then Rs. 475 per chair), offers a gift worth Rs. 100 with every chair. Suppose a clock as a gift. Apart from that guarantee of free repair of the chair for one year. His attitude was also very friendly, so he had goodwill also. (3 offers + goodwill).

3. Customers were very happy because, they just paid Rs. 475, but they got a chair + the gift worth Rs. 100 plus free repair offer.

4. The other shop was selling at Rs. 450 (but no any kind of offer)

5. Grandfather purchases the gift in wholesale for Rs. 50 per piece but the retail price was Rs. 100 (so for the customer the gift is worth Rs. 100).

Chair Retail Price: Rs. 500

Discounted Selling Price: Rs. 475

Wholesale Purchase Price Rs. 300

Profit Margin: 475-300 = Rs. 175

Deduct wholesale price per gift: Rs. 25

Now the final profit: Rs. 150 per chair.

The other shopkeeper also gets the chair for Rs. 300, selling at Rs. 450 and earns the same profit margin Rs. 150.

But Grandfather's extra "intelligence and wisdom" applied in his business generates him more business and customers with an equal profit margin.

When grandfather expired, his son took over it. He also continued to sell in the same way but his attitude was not friendly. Now fewer people were purchasing from grandfather's shop.

When his son expired, his grandson took over the business. He was unaware of the reason for giving gifts and guarantee of repair to the customer because the profit margin is the same, even if he gives any offer or not as the other shopkeeper.

So the grandson stopped the "intelligence and wisdom" the grandfather applied in his business, because of that gradually, the business slows down. A little bit, it was running because of the goodwill created by the grandfather.

Generation by generation the "secret wisdom and intelligence" applied in business diminishes and the grandson doesn't want to give any offer or discounts, no friendly relationship with the customer.

Now grandson will face many consequences and will suffer later in life when the luxury and facilities earned by grandfather and his father will decrease. Until now the comfort and facilities he was enjoying were earned by his grandfather and father. He was consuming it but did nothing to sustain it.

The above example explains in detail how the understanding of "wisdom and intelligence" of human living diminished generation by generation. Now everybody is running after comforts, luxury, money, properties, etc. Nobody is aware of the "wisdom and intelligence" to perform obligatory duties to sustain humanity and to bring up divinity within the human.

Even in today's world, if we can go back and see the habit and attitudes of our ancestors, it was extremely different than now. We are living with so many material comforts, but in ancient times, resources were limited, hence comforts were limited.

Like a secret transfer generation by generation, the secret of "wisdom and intelligence of selfless action" is also embedded within us. But we are unaware of it, because of our interest and involvement in more material desire.

Our incarnation will continue until we get to realize the "wisdom and intelligence" of selfless obligatory duties and activities.

Like in the above story, in the future the great-grandson has to regain the "secret wisdom and intelligence" which his great grandfather was applied in his business.

***

The whole universe is controlled by the Supreme with his rules. He is invisible, still manages everything. The universe is not started when we born and not going to end the day we die. It has existed, we entered here as a guest for a limited days stay - (say less than 100 years). Take the necessary items from nature to feed our bodies and to fulfill our necessities for our existence until we are alive. While we are here, we have to perform some duties and actions to purify our mind and senses towards soul purification to join the supreme.

Since we have a body and it is visible to us, we forget that we are only temporary guests here and unaware of the selfless duties and actions to be performed. Instead, we feel proud and with power and greed, will try to manage the world in our way. We will register the properties of God and will develop attachment and bondage with other creatures of Supreme.

***

Now, one of the most important parts of Gita from verses 4/7.

Whenever action of selfishness increases and selfless karma diminishes in the mind of people, to make them understand, Supreme manifests.

(In most of the books, the above quote is mentioned as to when goodness (dharma) declines and badness (adharma) increases in the world after many centuries God takes the body and manifests in the world.)

Fortunately, I am writing this book, during 21 days of lockdown and at home, to be safe from the coronavirus issue. So let's try to understand the above connecting with our life and clarifying the following questions :

1. God will manifest once, after many centuries, then what about us, who are living today.

2. In which century God will manifest.

3. What does it mean - ignorance, goodness (dharma) decreases, badness (adharma) increases?

4. Who are good people per God and who are bad people per God.

5. How God will identify and analyze, what and who is good & bad.

Answer to the above, in my way of understanding :

1. God will manifest in any form, for each one of us.

2. Anyday or every day to each one of us.

3. Goodness – all kinds of selfless actions, intelligence, duties, and activities you do (an increase of Satvik Gunas).

Badness - all kinds of selfish actions, duties, and activities you do (an increase of Tamas and Rajas Gunas).

4. Answered to above (3) is the answer.

5. According to your selfless and selfish actions per above.

Example :

The universal truth like birth and death are controlled by the Supreme itself. When, where, why it happened are unclear to humans. When the Supreme decides to change its Soul from one body to another, it finds its way. It may be natural or unnatural.

But in the above statement, God's manifestation is not to kill you.

Let's recall the story quoted earlier about Grandfather's store which was running successfully when grandfather was there. But now the store is handling by his great-grandson and the sale of the store is very low and the owner now (great-grandson) is suffering his life.

Why? – because of the righteousness, goodness, selfless action, dharma followed by the grandfather is diminished. The owner of today is unknown to the real secret of success the great-grandfather followed and it was successful those days. The store was transferred to generation by generation, so we are unknown to the fact that what exact trick of business was followed by the ancestors for success. The store was transferred to generation by generation, but the intelligence, wisdom, and the secret was not transferred. Transferring the same shop to generation by generation confirms, earlier it was successful, otherwise it was stopped at that time itself.

The new owner (the great-grandson), tried to renovate the store, more products added, but still, the result was low.

The store was earlier successful because of the goodwill, attitude and many other offers provided to the customers (selfless action) and the satisfied customers, again and again, visited the same shop.

But now the situation is different. Lost its success and his life is in trouble because he is dependent on the store for the livelihood and now the expenses, etc. are more than earlier.

The reason for the low performance of the store is called – badness, dharma, and selfish action – (new generation forgot and lost the intelligence and wisdom applied by his great-grandfather).

Then, how the goodness, dharma, selfless action can be established, how God will manifest.

When in extreme trouble, everything beyond our control, people surrender to God. Some go to check astrology, some go to various spiritual places or some go for counseling, etc.

Some people even suicide or getting into crime because of irritation, anger, etc.

Suppose, the great-grandson (the current owner of the shop), one day accidentally meets a person of this grandfather's age at someplace and this person knows his grandfather and heard about the attitude and selfless action followed by them to run the store. This aged person should this gentleman because the new generation losing their character, attitude, etc. and more selfish, lavish and no respect towards society. They even forgot the real duties and responsibilities to be performed to satisfy the creator.

So this aged person reveals the secret of his great-grandfather, and grandfather followed and makes him realize the dharma (selfless karma), goodness, etc. followed by them. The store is still surviving because of the little bit effect of their karma (selfless action) exists. The store was transferred to him by his ancestors, not built by him.

This aged person advises him to re-establish and follow the right action, selfless action, offer of discounts, friendly with customers, offers, etc. as followed by the great-grandfather.

Here the aged person represents Krishna who appeared before him to reveal the secret wisdom followed by his ancestors. Ultimately, instead of a person coming to advise, maybe we can get the wisdom from any book, or we can inspire by anybody's activity. If we came to know that a person in another city is more successful who also runs a shop like us. So, we can inspire from his actions.

There are various ways to manifest God to diminish the ignorance within you and transform wisdom and intelligence.

If somebody can follow the actions, attitude, intelligence and wisdom followed by Dr. APJ Abdul Kalam, anybody can become like him. If you follow at least 50% of it, 50% goodness you can experience in your life.

Overall, God will manifest in any form, just to realize the real secret and selfless action which you had forgot and because of that your sufferings.

God won't manifest the next day as the trouble starts. The diminishing of sales of that shop even started when his father was there, gradually the diminishing of sales increased and now the current owner is in extreme trouble, in confusion, in disappointment, what to do.

But now because of the help of an aged person, he got realized the mistakes he was following. Per his advice, he-regains the memory, know the secrets and re-establish righteousness in his attitude and the shop again runs successfully.

Both options were there – why God manifested to help him. Why doesn't God ruined him, punished him?

Because this person was in search of wisdom, goodness, and help. He has shown interest to find out ways to re-establish (Swatik Guna applied), hence he found and succeded.

But some people are adamant about their attitude (Tamasik and Rajasik guna was applied). Instead of finding solutions, they continued with their luxury life, choose to take more loans and try different businesses, selfish actions will continue and when all will fail, they will addict to alcohol, etc. Such people either suicide becomes drug addicts, mad and will ruin their life. His ego, adamant, etc. ruined him.

(God manifests means – getting the wisdom, understanding the divinity within you for righteousness actions, and to regain your memory of hidden selfless action and duties to be performed)

Nowhere to go for another example, whoever reads this, will understand the importance of Gita, who is Krishna, who is Arjuna and who is Duryodhana.

Arjuna was in doubt and confusion, finding for a solution –surrendered in front of God and has requested to help and guide. So Krishna advised him and revealed the secrets of wisdom and intelligence to overcome the problem.

Duryodhana was adamant in his attitude. He has no respect to Krishna, he was overconfident on his powers and was attracted to many un-wanted desires, ego, and attachments. Even Krishna was near to him too. But his and his brother's egoistic attitude ruined them, rather the ruined the whole kingdom.

Even in Ramayana, when Ram finally kills Ravana, Rama tells him "your ego killed you, not me – I was there to bring you up, many scholars had advised you to cut your ego and follow righteousness for the benefit of you and all, but you were adamant in your attitude which ultimately ruined you."

An important quote to note :

Dharma as mentioned in Mahabarata –" Dharanadharma ityahu: - dharmodhaarayati praja:

"One must do selfless, righteousness action towards obligatory duty in compliment to God and your followers will do the same.

Every action of us must be to clean our minds and to satisfy God to reach/achieve him.

Eg: Boss of your office in India, sent you to Australia to do some duties. But the expected result was not coming from you. You sent many fake reports and photos to him to show that you are working hard. Boss was still unsatisfactory and asked him to shift to Singapore and perform some other duties there. But again, the boss was unhappy because the expected result was not coming.

But the boss is always a boss.

Boss decided to visit Singapore without informing his staff there. He secretly reached his location but he was not there. He asked other people about him. They said, he was not performing the duties assigned to him and instead, he is enjoying most of his time in bars, beach with friends. Boss also saw it, but without disturbing him, the boss returned to India.

Later the boss asked him to return to India and join the duties here.

He came back after a few days and joined his duties.

The day he joined, the boss organized a meeting with all the employees of the company. In front of all the employees, the boss announced of terminating one of his employees who recently returned from the tour to Australia and Singapore. He will also be issued a breach of code-of-conduct of the company and bad conduct a certificate so that he cannot get a job anywhere else.

Everybody asked why the boss terminated him. The terminated employee even asked the boss, why he is terminated. He with an egoistic mind recalled the boss about his higher degrees, high family status, power, etc. and said he was perfect and truthful in his duties. Nobody was aware that the boss has visited Singapore and has already seen his performance live in Singapore, so the action is taken against him.

Instead of accepting and correcting his wrongdoings and ask for forgiveness to the boss, the employee fought with him and challenged him to show his success without the help of the boss, either working with other company or by establishing a new business set up as his own.

Since he has no previous work experience to show, all other companies rejected him. The previous company was terminated because of his shortcomings and though, they had given him a bad-conduct certificate which he cannot show anywhere.

He tried and tried, but he could not get a good job. Later he tried to establish his own business with the help of his father investing a big amount of money to satisfy his ego and to show his success to the other boss.

But forgot that he was terminated not because of lack of qualification, status, power, etc. but terminated because of his attitude, ego and for not performing the duties assigned to him by the boss. Instead, he was enjoying lavishly on company expenses, forgetting the boss who is spending money and duties for which he is sent to Australia and Singapore.

Anyway...his ego, attitude and selfish action collapsed him. He couldn't find a good job and lost in business with a loss of a huge amount of his father's savings. After the expiry of his father, he collapsed and lost everything even his house and properties. He was addicted to the drug. Later he shifted to another city and started to live like labour to survive

I think the above story well explained who is Krishna (Boss), Soul (Duryodhana), Power (his father), Selfish Action – Adharma (his attitude and actions), Power of Boss (termination), Effect of Karma (he ruined his life).

His degrees, power status – waste

Power of Boss applied and he collapsed.

If he understood the power of boss and surrenders him asking for his forgiveness, the boss might have forgiven, advised the right way to perform duties and actions and the boss might have helped him and he might be enjoying his life.

There is a quote in Sanskrit – "SAT-CHIT-ANAND"

Understand that truth (God – Boss), who is always after you, with you and within you in your heart. Since you know the truth, you will follow only good actions that will rejoice your heart.

Understand that God's power within you, perform duties complementary to him and feel the pleasure within you.

Even If anybody has any doubt and want that God has to manifest in every century to control greed, pride, and unrighteousness, just recall those days when the Coronavirus affected the whole world and every person. Nobody's power, greed, money, politics around the world, has worked.

***

.

Those who achieve without any doubt, the wisdom and understanding of Supreme, its power, and the duties and action assigned by him to us, never get a re-birth.

In the above story of boss and employee. After the termination, the employee tried his best to settle in another job and when failed tried to set up his own business to become a boss. But his actions disqualified him to become a boss. When he achieves all the qualities to become a boss, through his selfless action and duties, he will become a boss.

He will become a boss from an employee – Soul (employee) will join Krishna or become Krishna (Boss). Once the Soul joins the Supreme, no more the Soul exists. Only Krishna (boss) exists. (4/9).

***

There are so many people around the world who have achieved either the quality of Supreme or joined Supreme by the extreme practice of self-less karma, detachment from desires, etc.

Achieved Supreme means – Boss quality achieved (qualified with selfless divine qualities).

Joined Supreme means – The employee by achieving Boss qualities, partnered with Boss (two bosses in one company – both are partners – both of their actions, attitude and duties are the same). (4/10)

***

The concept of God is different for different people. Some find in pictures, some find in statues, some find in trees, some find in materials and their expectations are also different. Some worship for money, some for health, some for any other things. I manifest in their mind per their concept and their life also moves on per their concept only. Your life is the outcome of your concept about it.

I am very lazy – Yes you will become lazy.

I am smart – Yes, you will become smart.

I have problems – Yes you will have problems.

I am happy – Yes, you will be happy.

Now...

He is bad – Yes, for you – he is bad (for him he is good).

He is a cheater – Yes, for you - he is a cheater (not for him)

Those are bad people – Yes, for you, those are bad people.

He is characterless – Yes, for you, he is characterless.

That place is dirty – Yes, for you, that place is dirty.

It all depends on your thought and concept you have developed in your mind. You said, "he is wrong" – it doesn't mean that 'he is wrong' for the whole people around the world. It all depends on the clarify of your mind.

Sometimes on a sunny day, when we travel in the car, we can see some puddles of water on the road in some distance, but when we reached near to it, nothing was there. It was a misconception. It is called an optical phenomenon called mirage caused by the reflection of light rays due to different temperatures of the air above the road. (4/11).

A Quote to note :

You have a belief that you are a good person and are free from any evil thought and action.

But, still, let's see how the dirt or rust affects your mind and disturbs.

Suppose there is an alcoholic person resides nearby you and he is used to beating his wife. You didn't have a direct relationship with that family but you came to know about it through your servent. You have also shared it with your friends and very often you discuss it with your servent and friends. Most of the time in a day, whenever you think or speak about that alcoholic person, you are imagining him. If by chance, you are seeing that person on road, your mind fills with anger and revenge.

Now let's ask some questions...

Does he do something wrong with you? No.

Did you see that he is beating his wife? No.

Do you know, why he is an alcoholic? No.

Do you know about guna dominancy which reflects in one's actions? No.

Do you have any relationship with that family? No.

Do you like alcoholism? No.

Are you sure whether he is good or bad or do you have any authority to verify it? No.

You had believed that you are a good person with a clean mind. Let's confirm it.

Your discussion with your servent about other's family matters is not good for your mind.

You don't like alcoholism – but it is there in your mind whenever you discuss it.

You don't like the attitude of that person – but it is there in mind whenever you discuss his attitude.

You don't like that person – but his image is there in your mind.

Do you think that whether the above attitude of you, will be cultivating anything good in your mind?

They are good or not, it is not our business.

But we have dirted our mind whenever we think, image, discuss their matter. So many bad karmas we are doing this way and occupying a good part of the mind with such specks of dirt.

If we don't like something like alcoholism, we should not think, speak about it and don't even imagine or speak about his name.

Whenever we imagine, speak and discuss, his wrong habit of alcoholism, all of it (which we don't like) reflects in our mind.

When we achieve the wisdom of guna dominance, we will understand why the other person is an alcoholic and instead of showing anger or revenge on him, we will pity him.

If we don't like anybody's attitude, actions and even the person who possesses it, we should delete it from our mind, forget it and don't imagine or discuss it. They may or may not be good, it is their choice, the fruit in return for their doings decides the nature. We have no authority to check who is good or bad. Even by just thinking all about it, we dirt and disturb our minds.

In Gita – 12/13 – it says to practice "ADVESHTA SARVA BHOOTANAAM" - Let's love all, don't envious.

Just think the opposite, what would have been the effect in our mind, if we think, read, speak, imagine great scholars, intelligent people, great books, etc.

***

Those who expect the immediate result for their action, worship the divine creatures (devatas) under the Supreme.

I had already explained earlier, who will be a "divine creature or devata".

Suppose, you need a mango and to achieve it, if you sit and worship the Supreme, no mango will come. You have to either plant a tree and or to buy from a Mango Seller otherwise somebody gifts you.

You are the needy – then whoever provides you the blessing, is called "Devata".

When somebody approaches you for help if you are capable to help them and you bless them by providing help, at that time you are also a "Devata".

A "devata" can be a person, a thing, an invisible thing like air, sun, moon, water, food, tree, animals, etc. etc.

If one is capable of fulfills (or bless with) other's need – we respect such person or thing and called them "devata".

All the above things come under Supreme, but we directly expect the blessings from Supreme, it won't happen. If we need energy, we need to get it from Sun.

For example, President of a country is the Prime Administrator (Supreme) – but if you need a small help of road repair in your society, first you need to approach the local administrator (sub-administrator - devata) whom you can easily meet and he will bless you by providing the help. But if you insist to meet the President, even though he has higher power and authority, per protocol, you can't meet him for such a silly help.

***

Per the quality dominancy and talent within every human, they are classified as teachers, rulers, businessman and service providers. But the classifications of people based on their talent and expertise have later grouped and then originated the caste system.

Teachers and Scholars group - known as Brahmana

Leaders, Ministers, Rulers, Warrior – known as Kshatriya

Businessman for good & grains – Known as Vaishya

Service providers to all above – Known as Shoodra

If the group classifications are based on quality and talents, then the son of a teacher or a scholar cannot be called a teacher if he does not possess the quality, talent, and qualification as a teacher or scholar.

The son of a teacher or scholar may have an interest in doing business to earn money. He learns how to do business, partnering with a businessman and becomes a successful businessman. Shall we call him a 'teacher or scholar"? No.

The same happens in other classification also.

But a Teacher or Scholar need protection from Kshatriya (Ruler or warrior), Teacher and Ruler both need food and grains from Businessman (Vaishya) all three need service from Service Providers (Shoodra).

All need all.

Let me quote the story of an Air Hostess (Service Provider). She has a false belief that she deserves respect as a teacher because her father was a teacher irrespective of her actual talent and expertise she possesses. Once, one of the sweepers of the flight (Service Provider) invited her to a birthday party of his son. Immediately, her ego clashed and shouted on him how dare to invite her to be a sweeper.

Both were doing their duty as "Service Providers", she was serving food and water to passengers and the sweeper cleaning the flight.

She needs the expertise of a sweeper to clean – it means a sweeper is also important.

The Business Owner of the flight (comes under the Vaishya category), needs the expertise of both Air Hostess and Sweeper.

The Minister needs a flight to travel with the help of Piolet, Air Hostess and Sweeper.

The Teacher also requires the help of all the above.

All of them have equal importance in our life because we all need each one's service, help, and support for our smooth life.

A businessman who runs a construction company has to depend on hundreds and thousands of experts from various fields to run his construction business. No buildings can be constructed just showing or throwing money, experts needed to work on. He also needs a customer to buy his flats or building. It may be a minister who buys his flat. Just imagine those workers of cleaning of sewage systems, we can hire him paying mone, everyone can be hired even a big person or small person. Minister hired builder for flats, builder hired various experts to build the house, those experts hires laborers, sweepers, etc. Money is the necessity of each one on the earth. But shall everyone can do everyone's work. Shall a builder do the work of a sweeper? The work of a sweeper or a sewage cleaner is not easy, and apart from that they sweep and clean the dirt we did. What we dirtied, they clean. Then, who is important "the one who dirtied" or "the one who clean". Everyone depends on one another.

So, the classification by the caste system is baseless. Nowadays it has been used by politicians or some groups of people for their personal and political gains.

An Important quote to note :

What is mentioned above is the situation among humans through mind and senses and quality (guna) dominance within it? Not to misunderstand that the Supreme (Krishna) also possesses all the same qualities as a human. Even being the creator of mind and senses with various gunas in it, Supreme doesn't possess it and thus no such discriminatory attitude by it. Means for God, we all are the same. All good and bad happens with us by the action and attitude based on guna dominancy.

One more way to understand the category and divisions connecting with the human body :

Brain – thinking - intelligence - Brahmana

Hands & Chest – do the works – actions - Kshatriya

Stomach – Food digestion and distribution - Vaishya

Legs – helps to stand – Shoodra

There are many trees, but its look, leaf, fruit, taste all are different, and the same with animals, birds, etc. (4/14)

***

The Supreme and any other creature on earth except humans do nothing with any kind of expectation in return. That's why they don't possess any kind of bondage, attachment, desire for any material things.

Those humans who know this concept and follow it, won't attract, attach or develop any kind of bondage with any physical or material things and will be free from any fear of loss. (4/14).

The ancient saints (rishis) also followed the same pathway as above, thus they have developed wisdom and intelligence, and with it, they were able to discover many universal secrets and paved the way to light up the world with knowledge.

Wisdom and intelligence of those people are hidden because of their engagement in selfish action, bondage, attachment anger, jealousy and desire on material things, etc. Most such people will end their life in grief, disappointments, and fear of loss.

But those understood the value of selfless action, such wisdom achieved personalities open up their multiple talents, capabilities, etc. and contribute many things through discoveries, inventions, etc. for the benefit of the people around the world. Eg: Dr. APJ Abdul Kalam, Mahatma Gandhi, Pandit Madan Mohan Malviya, Albert Einstein, Swami Vivekananda, Vinoba Bhave, etc. (4/15)

***

There are three important things about action (karma) are explained, *(1) Actions (Karma), Purity and Intention of Action (vikarma) & inaction (akarma).*

***What is action (Karma)*(visible action)** – we have
already explained this in the previous chapter and had
divided it based on the intention of action we perform as
selfish (Kriya) and selfless (karma).

Both selfish and selfless karma is required.

To feed the family and for their well being, we need to do
a lot of karmas which we called "Kriya – selfish based
karma" because of the intention, "for me and my family
only" with extreme attachment.

The intention of Karma (Vikarma) –
happens within mind

Vikarma or intention of Karma is like the essence of every
action like lime juice with sweet and lime juice with salt.
Lime juice is like an action (karma) and its tastes are like
good intentions and bad intentions based on the
ingredient (salt-sugar) we mix on it. If we mix sugar
(good intention), it will taste sweet and if we mix salt
(bad intention), it will taste salty.

Only water and lime are not enough, to taste it either
sweet or salt as ingredients you need to mix on it.

To light up an oil lamp, only oil and a wick made of cotton
is not enough. We need to light up with a match stick.
Lighting up a lamp with a match stick is a good action
because its light removes dark.

Let's deeply understand the same action, at a different level. There are two lamps of light in a small house where there is no electricity. Even though light removes darkness, here there are different intentions of lighting up of two different lamps. One lamp is lighting up with kerosene and the other one is lighting up with ghee (clarified butter). The action and intention behind both the light are good.

Still, the intention of lighting up one of the lights is of a more purified nature. Why both are not of kerosene, why one is with clarified butter.

The light of kerosene to remove the dark of outside and the light of clarified butter is to remove the dark of your inside.

The light of kerosene is to light up the room and the light of ghee (clarified butter) is for the pooja room (meditation room). The fact, reason, and intention behind lighting up the lamp with ghee (clarified butter) is not to light up the pooja room rather light up our Soul.

If you have any health problem and you need a massage. A professional by payment doing it and your mother doing it. Whose touch with be divine and pure. I think no need to mention.

When in every action, the purity of intention lights up your mind and thus the intelligence and wisdom develop towards union with Supreme.

Those who perform fasting etc., outside they do all purification, light up lamps, will do mantra chanting, etc., but the same if not happening internally, no use of fasting because the ultimate reason of performing pooja, fasting, etc. is to clean and purify the mind so whatever we do outside must happen internally too. While doing it, we are connected with body and mind, connected with Soul and Supreme that's why in India it is called "Upasana" means sitting with God or being with God.

***

For example, suppose, it is our habit of making jokes, abusing when among friends, but what would happen if one of our great teacher or a great scholar or even our father come nearby us. We will maintain silence and exchange meaningful, thoughtful, respectful talking among all.

While doing Rudra Abhishek, the water is falling on a shiv linga and it purifies, but if the internal purification of mind and senses (good intention as water) is not happening, then there is no use of that pooja. We and the Shiv linga both are just a stone.

An important quote to note :

Once in a temple, a rich person of the city with his bodyguards has come for worship. Every movement of him has reflected the ego he carries being a rich person. He was also wandering here and there to check whether anybody is noticing him or not. He has submitted a big bundle of sweet and big garlands inside. After taking a few sweets for the submission to the deity, the rest of the sweets returned to him by the Pandit as Prasad "sacred food". After his worship, while returning, he distributed some sweets to some people and scholars who were chanting mantras over there. One of the scholars who was watching all of his activities refused to take his sweet. Later one scholar asked the other scholar who refused to take his sweet (Prasad) the reason for rejecting it. Then the scholar said, "his body saluted the deity with folded hands – but not his mind".

We salute the divine by bending with folded hands in front of a statue or picture of God, but complete devotion from a purified my happens when the mind also bends inside, in the same way, we do outside. Salute and pray the divine with an egoistic mind doesn't make any purpose of pooja or worshipping.

Selfless karma with good intention happens when we do service both by hand (action) and heart (sacrifice) like we perform pooja by hand outside and by heart inside.

Some examples of karma and intention

1. When we do some help to someone by selfless karma (helping an outsider), but there is an intention behind it that they must thank us or help us back when we are in need.

2. We do selfless karma (not to relatives, outsiders) – but want to take a photo and put it on Facebook to show up the public.

3. Visited in a bulk tree plantation event, took a photo of plantation and gone back. No contribution to buy new seeds, no help for further cultivation and no intention of what would happen with the plants which are planted now. The whole interest was to show up that we are a tree lover.

4. Visited hospital to serve through an NGO, but there is no mercy or kindness in mind towards the patient there.

5. Some people are engaged in social service opening an NGO. They will publish them that they are going to serve the public wholeheartedly. They will contact different people for contributions, but if few are not contributing them, they will abuse them. Recently on Facebook, I have seen a person who runs an NGO to feed food to poor people. He has already shown his bank account details near to his profile picture at the top and through a video, he is demanding contributions. But he has got fewer contributions as he was expected. Next day he has streamed another Facebook live video, abusing the whole people who have not contributed and apart from that in the same video, he is praying God to disturb the life of all people who have not contributed so that people can suffer and understand the feeling of hunger, etc.

Nobody asked him to open an NGO. Every city there are hundreds of NGOs and most of the people contribute something, fewer or higher per their capacity to the needy. However, one has to contribute or not, it depends on them, we are nobody to pressurize and curse, if not contributed.

If you are starting a charity organization, you must have the capacity to run it and serve the people. Not to start an NGO with the expectation that others will contribute. They may or may not be contributing.

Akarma (inaction) -

"SHAANTAAKAARAM BHUJAGA SHAYANAM"

The Supreme, the Creator– managing the whole universe and its creatures, but still silently in a serene appearance with the embodiment of peace rested on a serpent.

Some action (karma) did by somebody, but the credit of it even not felt in his mind and even nobody knew about it. He did everything and did nothing (felt or happened nothing).

It is one of the highly purified states of mind and achiever of higher spiritual development. It happens when one achieves the wisdom of nothingness.

For example: when you were walking through a village in the evening, you are seeing that an alcoholic father throws the painting of his daughter outside saying that he doesn't like the paintings, there is no value to it, so either concentrate on household things, earn money or get ready for marriage.

You have collected a few of those paintings without their notice and felt excellent. So you decide to help that girl without any information to them that you are helping them.

You have contacted one of your foreign friends residing in the same city who collects painting etc. and by explaining the situation, asked her to visit the village, visit the house of that painting artist, appreciate her art and buy some paintings. You also asked her to buy some paintings for you. But you didn't visit the house of the artist.

In the next few days, the foreigner girl visits the house of the artist, appreciates her work, buy something and giving the money to her father. The foreigner also told the father that she will again come to collect more and more so do more paintings. Her father was astonished and was very happy. His daughter was allowed to continue painting and started love her, respect and support her work.

Very often, once or twice a month, either a foreigner or any other friend of you visited the house of artist and used to buy her paintings.

Either way, you established an artist's talent and brought harmony to the family.

All the action was done by yourself, but you never shared it with anybody in the village, not to your friends and not published it anywhere. Even in your face, it was not reflected. Sometimes you meet his father in the market and you even speak with him, but the father doesn't know that you are helping his family and you ever tried to show up.

You are relaxed, quiet and calm like the Supreme resting in the ocean under serpent's shadow. This is called "inaction" – it occurs when one has achieved a complete detachment on every physical and material detachment.

*****

An Important quote to note :

Inaction is also karma (action) which you did but you immediately deleted all of its credit from your mind, like you draw a line on the water which is disappeared immediately or you wrote something on the board and wiped off immediately.

*****

The complete sacrifice of everything like name, fame, attitude like me, mine, why should I, for what, for whom, what I get, etc. are required to perform such action, the truthful selfless action. (4/16-23).

Every such action has a Soul to Soul connection or Soul to Supreme Connection or Supreme to Supreme connection. It's like a prayer that "Everything created by you including me, submitting that everything to you".

The world is yours, every creature is yours, my body is yours, all physical and material things are yours, so if I help somebody with anything from nature, it belongs to you, even the something and somebody belongs to you or you are the ultimate authority of everything. Then how can one say, it's me, mine, I did, for me, etc. (4/24).

Just imagine the mental satisfaction of those people, who follow such a great fire of sacrificing in every action as mentioned above. It is called "Divine's satisfaction of a cleaned mind" (4/25).

***

People follow different pathways to attain divine wisdom and intelligence by facing and chasing different situations in life.

1. Trying to control what they listen through the ear and what they speak through the mouth. Avoid listening and reacting to negative things, abuses, etc. and also avoid speaking negative things about something or somebody, and also abuse and condemn them.

2. Trying to avoid a fight if somebody abuse, condemn one by maintaining silence, forgiving or staying away from those people and adverse situations. He will try to burn the agony, feelings, and thoughts by the fire of intelligence and wisdom or submit to Supreme. 4/27

(The power of speech, words, and sound and its effects are explained in Chapter 16) – (Verses 16/18).

An important quote to note :

Mahatma Gandhi said: "If someone slaps you on the one side of your face, turn the other one to him"

What does it mean? Does he advise us to take more slaps on our face or does it has a cool meaning?

Let's understand this through an example :

One day in the morning, suppose you are going to attend the most important business meeting with your client from abroad in your car. While crossing a traffic signal on the road, a boy with a new bike hits on the front right side of your car. A small hit mark is there. By the look, he is an illiterate guy from a poor background. You were perfect on your driving and the whole error happened because he was coming from the wrong side. It is his mistake completely, but the boy looking at you in anger that you did the mistake.

How you will react in this situation. Are you going to get down and fight with him? Are you going to teach him the traffic rules? If you try to do all this, you are going to lose many things, but nothing will happen to him.

If you raise your anger and fights there, it will be going to reflect in the business meeting which is going to hold after a while. You will feel full of anger and distress and it will remain for a day or few days. That boy may come later to you with more of his friends to fight with you.

But if you are intelligent, you can manage the situation within no time.

As the bike hits your car, considering your status and his status, considering your emergency of going and to maintain peace of mind, you immediately look at him for a second, give a smile, raise your hand and by action, you say "its okay, no issue, leave it" and immediately moves your car towards the destination.

Within a second, you managed the situation.

What actually happened here? Instead of winning him, you win the situation.

In a few seconds, you forget the situation whatever happened and you have started imagining how to present in the meeting, etc.

Here you surrender to win the situation.

Surrendering in such a situation is called "as showing your other side of your face".

Everybody has two sides of a face. Even that boy also has it.

He has shown one of his faces by hitting you by ignorance. You also had two options to show both sides of your faces. Either you show one side of your face with anger or show the other side of your face by forgiving him.

Wisely choose one to win the situation and to maintain peace in mind.

***

Continuing from above....

3. Some people distribute food and grains to needy without notice to anybody towards their sacrifice and action.

4. Some people constantly stick to their actions concentrating their mind on their work. They don't involve in other's matter and life and don't try to intervene in anybody's matter unnecessarily. It is like even not watching TV serials and new debates.

5. Some people concentrate their minds on reading and writing for the benefit of future generations.

6. Some people will practice regular meditations to maintain pure breathing inside by pushing out bad energies.

7. Some people control their food habits. Earlier they might have eaten a lot. But now when they are on the pathway to achieving wisdom, they controls it and has developed simple food habit. Earlier it was like "living for food", now "food for living". So required that much only for self-sustain. Simple food, healthy living. (4/31)

The importance of the above is explained in detail in Chapter-14)

***

Who takes/consumes the rest/balance after sacrifice who attains Supreme satisfaction. This was already explained earlier with the example of mother who prepares food, serves everybody in the family and consumes the leftover. Her satisfaction is more than that of other family members who had tasted everything fresh.

Another example is the shopkeeper who runs a shop to serve people and not to earn money only. Both shopkeepers will get profit, but one shopkeeper is not worried about it. Let the customers be happy, I am happy with whatever profit comes. He sacrifices/deletes the desire from the mind that how much I will earn, instead feeds the mind, how best I can serve people.

Those who sacrifice such material desires will be happy, satisfactory and will maintain permanent peace of mind.

Those who have an attachment to material desires will always like narrow-minded, always feel fear of loss, no peace, and satisfaction. (4/31)

***

As explained above, there are various methods of sincere selfless action with self-sacrifice explained in ancient literature like Vedas, etc. and had also followed by many of our ancestors. (4/33).

***

We have gone through the different kinds of actions, the importance of selfless action, sacrifice and various other ways to achieve wisdom and intelligence so far.

But to easily achieve and make us understand the wisdom, we need an excellent teacher (Guru), who has all the above qualities. No all saints who are in saffron dress, not all priests, not all scholars are qualified to teach.

The Saint, Scholar, or a Teacher (Guru) – must have all those qualities as we explained earlier.

If a Guru is preaching for publicity, media attention, enjoying a lavish lifestyle, has anger in attitude, has the desire and attachment in physical and material things, then he cannot be a perfect Guru. He is just like a common man who enjoys a normal lifestyle without having any universal knowledge and wisdom.

But a perfect Guru must have no desires in anything. His main motto will be to satisfy the Supreme and deliver the teachings to those eager students who have complete dedication to attain wisdom and intelligence. It is not the student who actually finds the Guru, but the Guru will identify the dedicated student among various students.

If a student wants to become a doctor, the student has to qualify various examinations then only he/she is being selected for that. Thousands of students are trying for that and only a few get the admission.

In the same way, the Teacher/Guru selects his disciple per their dedication and interest towards attaining wisdom and intelligence.

The disciple should also have full confidence over the quality of the Teacher before finalizing because once you become a disciple of a teacher, you must follow him/her undoubtedly.

For a teacher to deliver the teachings to the disciple, he/she has to show his/her complete sincere devotion, eagerness and dedication towards learning, simplicity in asking questions and make the teacher happy by doing various services. Depending on your devotion and dedication, the Teacher will gradually clear your doubts and transfer the wisdom which he has been achieved. Just like there are examinations in school or college to qualify the next level, the teacher will also test you in various ways to check your dedication and to deliver further teachings.

That's why in Kathopanishad (1.3.14), it mentions – getting the universal teachings from a good teacher is not that easy and it will be like traveling on a sharp razor.

That disciple who achieves the wisdom and intelligence will be free from any kind of bondage or attachment with any physical or material things, the selfish me-mine attitude will also be removed. Then he will see the whole universe within him and also in Supreme. (4/35).

(Please refer Chapter – 9 to understand in detail how one can see the whole universe within him – what does it mean?)

Wisdom and intelligence are like soap and washing powder which cleans the dirt in cloths. Through continuous teaching by different examples, clearing the doubts in mind is like cleaning dirt from cloths using different soap and washing powder. Some dirts may be of very old and so tough to remove, then we use different cleaning solutions other than soap and washing powder.

How the different cleaning solutions clean the dirt of clothes even if it is tough or older, the wisdom and intelligence will clean the dirt of mind even if it is generated from a previous birth or previous years of this birth.

Wisdom and intelligence clean all the sins you have generated, like the fire burns the wood into ashes.

Like there is nothing other than the fire that can burn/purify any physical material, there is nothing other than wisdom and intelligence which can burn the sins and dirt of our mind.

All those wisdom achieved disciples who are sincere, selfless, dedicated, devoted, eager, free from desires, detached from physical and material attachment, achieved mental balancing will get permanent peace and experience the Supreme within the self. (4/38-39).

***

Now let us discuss some other group of people in the society they are called – Suspicious People. (4/40)

One being suspicious always is also a kind of dirt which affects the mind. It makes one restless, distress, disappointed and unpeaceful.

Let's recall the name of the first chapter once again "Arjuna Vishada Yoga – Despondency of Arjuna or The Disappointed Arjuna or The warrior called Arjuna is in depression"

***

Medical science says suspicion happens when you experience paranoia anxiety, depression or low self-esteem. It may be more likely to experience paranoid thoughts – or be more upset by them.

Per Wikipedia - Suspicion is cognition of mistrust in which a person doubts the honesty of another person or believes another person to be guilty of some type of wrongdoing or crime, but without sure proof.

***

Per the teaching of Acharya Vinoba Bhave, for suspicious people, the Supreme (Krishna) is on the other side of a mountain. Whatever deity or God the worship, whatever actions they person but they still needed to clean the whole mountain of dirt (suspicious mind) to visualize/experience the Supreme.

There are various reasons for one being suspicious like Jealousy, not meeting the expectation one has with other, fixed thought of one being a culprit, fear of loss, feeling of un-acceptance, unexpected growth of somebody from common to extra-ordinary, one's relation with a various group of people in the society, one's detachment with family relations and more engagement with the society, etc.

An atheist who doesn't believe in the existence of God is also a suspicious person.

Let us remember the famous quote of Abraham Lincoln - "Believing everybody is dangerous, but believing nobody is more dangerous."

One of the famous American Moral and Social Philosopher Mr. Eric Hoffer says that the suspicious mind believes more than it doubts. It believes in a formidable and ineradicable evil lurking in every person.

There are so many people around the world with a belief that reading Bhagavad Gita makes one a saint. This false belief happens because of suspicious mentality. Arjuna's response to Krishna in Gita-18/73 clarifies it.

A suspicious mind is like a little boy who has lost in the crowd. He is unsure about the route to go back. He is wandering here and there. He lost his journey in between. He is unclear about the destination where he has to go. He has lost the peace in mind. He is abusing, crying, hitting people, throwing everything.

If he does not find a guide and is not properly guided, his life becomes miserable. His suspicious, unpeaceful mind will cultivate evil thoughts, anger, revenge, etc. in mind and will force him to do many evil actions, crimes, etc. and it may later lead to developing the mental disorder and many other health problems.

Those who are of suspicious nature, never find peace in mind, not even in this birth and not in the next.

There are many examples already given earlier about balancing the mind. The suspicious nature also develops because of ignorance of guna dominance.

Being suspicious is because of "tamasik and rajasik guna" dominance.

Being suspicious always is not a good activity (dirt in mind) as mentioned above like a boy lost in the crowd.

Then we need to apply high grade soap and washing powder as wisdom and intelligence to clean our mind.

You are perfect and want to do good things, but the dirt in your mind takes you to do the opposite.

A person should understand that "a suspicious mind" will disturb him only. Whatever actions will be developed from a suspicious mind will be of evil nature (rajasik and tamasik). The mind will be forced always to take revenge, hurt somebody, disturb somebody, abuse, condemn and spoil somebody.

If hundreds of good qualities are there in one person, the person with the suspicious mind will always try to dig to find the wrong qualities of that person and whatever action he does, will be negatively projected. This happens because of ignorance and unawareness about what guna dominance in each person.

If a suspicious person blames that the other person is a regular alcoholic. (okay – accepted, because of "rajasik and tamasik" guna dominance within him, he is alcoholic). But if you are suspicious with it, you also possess the same "rajasik and tamasik" guna dominance.

We are nobody to evaluate the actions of others. They are self-responsible for their actions. The fruit of one's action depends on their intention per guna dominance – "one reaps what he/she sew".

Suppose a person who feels jealousy of one's victory, then what would happen? The flames of jealousy and suspicion will burn the jealous person. Nothing is going to happen to the other person.

If one has a suspicious behavior between two relationships, then no sincere relationship exists in between. If somebody is forced to move with the relationship, it will be just mechanical.

If the brother is suspicious of the sister, the sister is suspicious of the brother, the father suspicious of the mother, the mother suspicious of the father and the father is suspicious of son or daughter. One's nature of suspicion kills the true relation.

I wish to narrate my own story on this.

During 1996 when I was working in a fan making company and I had a girlfriend. My parents disliked the relation so there were a lot of issues at home with it. She is also studying and stays in a hostel. Saturday evening or Sunday only she can meet anybody even to her parents. Once in a fortnight, we used to meet depending my office hours. Normal office time is 9 AM to 6 PM but being in a private company most of the days, we leave after 8 PM or so and reach home by 9 PM or maybe later.

Since the day, my parents knew that I have a girlfriend, the suspicion of my late coming has started. Every day in the evening when I reach, they used to scold me because of my late coming. I used to say, I am late because I left the office late. But their suspicious mind never believed my words.

The situation was like the proverb – "You can't wake a person that is pretending to be asleep".

So, because of the suspicious mind, one day my father visited the office to make a complaint to the manager about my late coming. The manager has convinced my father by explaining the reality and said to him that almost all the staff of the company leaves after 8 PM.

***

The people who have achieved wisdom and intelligence will remove the nature of being suspicious to avoid any kind of unpleasant happenings in their life. Without removing it, the mind will remain like a lost child in the crowd, develop evil thoughts and thus all activities, thought process will disturb.

One's mind must be like a prayer hall or a pooja room. Does anybody spit on the pooja room where you worship the divine? We throw the waste and garbage outside of the house, keeping it inside will generate bad smell, worms, bacteria, etc.

So one should try to clean the mind free of suspicion to smell good, do good and develop wisdom and intelligence.

***

Then what about the person who is a victim of a suspicious person. As I explained earlier in my story, my parents are suspicious of me because of my late arrival and they scold me regularly.

If satwik guna is dominated within me, I will be cool and silent. If "tamasik and rajasik" guna dominates within me, I will react and there will fight every day and there is no mental peace or mental balancing to anybody and no harmony at home.

But those who practice spiritual development by achieving wisdom and intelligence under a Guru or through reading books like Gita, etc. won't react to any abuses, condemnation, etc. by suspicious people, because he gets the wisdom of being in silence whenever such situations are there.

There is a saying in Sanskrit "manunam vidvaanu bhooshanam" – it means "silence is like a jewel for scholars". A wise should remain silent, while in the company of fools. Silence is the higher virtue.

There is a deep divine secret of the importance of being in silence which will be explained in Chapter 16/18 (why we should be very careful when we abuse anybody)

Let me quote a story which one of my friends Ankita narrated to me :

Ankita was a research scholar and was researching various dance forms of India, visited Chennai to stay with a male teacher of Bharatnatyam for a few months. She was from Orissa. Since the teacher is a renowned dancer and very famous among dancers of India, she chosen him to research. He is a Professor at a university there. He has a down to earth nature, creative and his attitude was quite impressive. Even in Orissa, people discuss his multi-talent personality, care, and simplicity in attitude.

After a few weeks of her staying there, to her surprise, she smelled something awkward there. It was the attitude of his wife. She was behaving very politely and rudely with him like he is the worst person in the society. She also runs a small Bharatnatyam School as her own but she is not famous like her husband.

The world around was appreciating him but she was abusing and condemning him.

But again it was surprised Ankita that she never sees him reacting or responding to his wife for her rude actions. He was sitting like a deaf and never reacted or uttered a word to respond. He maintained perfect silence and was always maintained a smile on his face. Nobody can understand that he is facing such a storm every day at home.

Ankita felt very bad about it, but she never asked about it to the teacher during her research.

After a few months, after completion of her research on that particular form of dance, she has to leave Chennai.

She thanked the teacher for the help and she has gifted something to the teacher towards a token of gratitude for the wonderful care and teachings she received during her stay. She felt lucky to have him.

The last day, before she leaves, she asked special permission to the teacher to meet him in the university office to discuss something. The teacher allowed it.

She asked him, why his wife behaves like this and how he will be able to face it so silently. She asked this question in a way like a Spiritual Disciple asking a Spiritual Scholar for wisdom.

Since a secret of mind management was there, the teacher decided to explain it to her.

He said that he is a Bharatnatyam Dancer, Professor of a University and most of his students are girls. Among so many students, a few are more talented, more dedicated and grasp the teaching so well. We used to select such students to do the lead role of group dance. We need to specially train them and need to spend more time with them than the other students. His closeness, care and attention with few particular students have developed doubt in his wife's mind and she became suspicious. But it was part of his job. Apart from that because of his special talent and his applying many creativity in his dance form he became very famous also. More and more people started liking him and his followers increased in and around the world. He was an inspiration for every new dance students. He used multiple innovative methods of teaching and that's why most of the students wanted to learn *dance under him. He also used to bear the fees of some talented students from his salary who were on the verge of stop learning because of poor finance.*

The suspicious mind of his wife never given any value to his growth, followers, name, fame, etc. and used to disturb him by abusing regularly. She started scripting stories about his relationship with students, spread rumors and tried her best to defame him and defame some of his students.

But he faced all those situations very silently, little bit disturbances happened to him initially but later he managed it with his power of balancing the mind. Luckily, he was the follower of Ramana Maharshi and used to read his books and that's why he understood the importance of mind balancing and a secret behind it. Even though his wife had thousands of complaints about him, outside among people, he was loved by everyone and was happy with his attitude, care, knowledge, and behavior. Everyone respected him because of his selfless service and attitude. If he had any characterless attitude, it would have reflected in his actions by now and the society might have responded to it.

He also said that if his mental balance disturbs, his teachings will disturb, his students will disturb, he will go in depression or disappointments. Because of one person's attitude, why we should disturb our mind. She wants to satisfy her suspicious mind by showing up that he is nothing for her, useless, valueless, etc. If he reacts, she will speak more, if he maintains silence she will speak less. Responding to those people is like pouring ghee (clarified butter), on the fire.

Per the teaching of Ramana Maharshi, if any bad karma of abusing others has been generated by the teacher in his past birth, he has to face it back in this birth. If he keeps silent, one day it will end. But if he reacts to it, he is adding more into it and instead of thousand, it will be more than a thousand to face. When we react, she will generate more bad karma by abusing more and more to win you.

As we explained earlier about the quote of Mahatma Gandhi to show the other face to slap means we want to win the situation and not the person.

If we maintain a dirt-free mind with good thoughts, wisdom, attitude, multi-talent, and intelligence, when we die, a clean, peaceful mind and senses with all that good qualities and developed talents will be carried forward to the next level of birth.

But if the whole life we abuse and condemn others, with anger, revenge, etc. a lot of bad karma will be generated throughout life and a highly dirtied, unpeaceful mind and senses will be carried forward with a bundle of bad karma to face in the next level of birth. No worshipping of God by such people with a mind full of anger, revenge, and curses will reap any result.

Ankita's respect towards the teacher was increased, it was like achieving wisdom from a Spiritual Guru. She touched his feet for his blessings and left the place with a relaxed mind. For Ankita, his teaching was like a bonus to her. (4/40).

So to achieve wisdom and intelligence by removing ignorance, one should be very careful in every activity by word, mind, and actions. Keep reading great books and follow the pathways of wisdom achieved scholars and try to control the mind and senses from wandering over physical and material desires. Good action or ill action – can be recognized when one keeps a constant vigil (wakeful state) during the wakeful state. Chapter-16 explains it.

Still, the ultimate secret practiced by wise scholars of being in silence if somebody abuses, condemns, etc. is revealed in Chapter 16 of this book by Bhagavad Gita verses 16/18.

Those who removed ignorance, doubts, suspicion from the mind by wisdom and intelligence never develop bondage or attachment for the action done by his body (4/41).

So let's cut all specks of dirt like ego, ignorance, doubts, anger, revenge, selfishness, etc. by the sword of wisdom so that we can practice selfless action towards obligatory duties in compliment to Supreme and develop self to the higher level of intelligence.

English Text of Chapter-4 Sanskrit Slokas for Quick Reference

1.

śhrī bhagavān uvācha

imaṁ vivasvate yogaṁ proktavān aham avyayam

vivasvān manave prāha manur ikṣhvākave 'bravīt

2.

evaṁ paramparā-prāptam imaṁ rājarṣhayo viduḥ

sa kāleneha mahatā yogo naṣhṭaḥ parantapa

3.

sa evāyaṁ mayā te 'dya yogaḥ proktaḥ purātanaḥ

bhakto 'si me sakhā cheti rahasyaṁ hyetad uttamam

4.

arjuna uvācha

aparaṁ bhavato janma paraṁ janma vivasvataḥ

katham etad vijānīyāṁ tvam ādau proktavān iti

5.

śhrī bhagavān uvācha

bahūni me vyatītāni janmāni tava chārjuna

tānyahaṁ veda sarvāṇi na tvaṁ vettha parantapa

6.

ajo 'pi sannavyayātmā bhūtānām īśhvaro 'pi san

prakṛitiṁ svām adhiṣhṭhāya sambhavāmyātma-māyayā

7.

yadā yadā hi dharmasya glānir bhavati bhārata

abhyutthānam adharmasya tadātmānaṁ sṛijāmyaham

8.

paritrāṇāya sādhūnāṁ vināśhāya cha duṣhkṛitām

dharma-sansthāpanārthāya sambhavāmi yuge yuge

9.

janma karma cha me divyam evaṁ yo vetti tattvataḥ

tyaktvā dehaṁ punar janma naiti mām eti so 'rjuna

10.

vīta-rāga-bhaya-krodhā man-mayā mām upāśhritāḥ

bahavo jñāna-tapasā pūtā mad-bhāvam āgatāḥ

11.

ye yathā māṁ prapadyante tāns tathaiva bhajāmyaham

mama vartmānuvartante manuṣhyāḥ pārtha sarvaśhaḥ

12.

kāṅkṣhantaḥ karmaṇāṁ siddhiṁ yajanta iha devatāḥ

kṣhipraṁ hi mānuṣhe loke siddhir bhavati karmajā

13.

chātur-varṇyaṁ mayā sṛiṣhṭaṁ guṇa-karma-vibhāgaśhaḥ

tasya kartāram api māṁ viddhyakartāram avyayam

14.

na māṁ karmāṇi limpanti na me karma-phale spṛihā

iti māṁ yo 'bhijānāti karmabhir na sa badhyate

15.

evaṁ jñātvā kṛitaṁ karma pūrvair api mumukṣhubhiḥ

kuru karmaiva tasmāttvaṁ pūrvaiḥ pūrvataraṁ kṛitam

16.

kiṁ karma kim akarmeti kavayo 'pyatra mohitāḥ

tat te karma pravakṣhyāmi yaj jñātvā mokṣhyase 'śhubhāt

17.

karmaṇo hyapi boddhavyaṁ boddhavyaṁ cha vikarmaṇah

akarmaṇaśh cha boddhavyaṁ gahanā karmaṇo gatiḥ

18.

karmaṇyakarma yaḥ paśhyed akarmaṇi cha karma yaḥ

sa buddhimān manuṣhyeṣhu sa yuktaḥ kṛitsna-karma-kṛit

19.

yasya sarve samārambhāḥ kāma-saṅkalpa-varjitāḥ

jñānāgni-dagdha-karmāṇaṁ tam āhuḥ paṇḍitaṁ budhāḥ

20.

tyaktvā karma-phalāsaṅgaṁ nitya-tṛipto nirāśhrayaḥ

karmaṇyabhipravṛitto 'pi naiva kiñchit karoti saḥ

21.

nirāśhīr yata-chittātmā tyakta-sarva-parigrahaḥ

śārīraṁ kevalaṁ karma kurvan nāpnoti kilbiṣham

22.

yadṛichchhā-lābha-santuṣhṭo dvandvātīto vimatsaraḥ

samaḥ siddhāvasiddhau cha kṛitvāpi na nibadhyate

23.

gata-saṅgasya muktasya jñānāvasthita-chetasaḥ

yajñāyācharataḥ karma samagraṁ pravilīyate

24.

brahmārpaṇaṁ brahma havir brahmāgnau brahmaṇā hutam

brahmaiva tena gantavyaṁ brahma-karma-samādhinā

25.

daivam evāpare yajñaṁ yoginaḥ paryupāsate

brahmāgnāvapare yajñaṁ yajñenaivopajuhvati

26.

śhrotrādīnīndriyāṇyanye sanyamāgniṣhu juhvati

śhabdādīn viṣhayānanya indriyāgniṣhu juhvati

27.

sarvāṇīndriya-karmāṇi prāṇa-karmāṇi chāpare

ātma-sanyama-yogāgnau juhvati jñāna-dīpite

28.

dravya-yajñās tapo-yajñā yoga-yajñās tathāpare

swādhyāya-jñāna-yajñāsh cha yatayaḥ sanśhita-vratāḥ

29-30.

apāne juhvati prāṇaṁ prāṇe 'pānaṁ tathāpare

prāṇāpāna-gatī ruddhvā prāṇāyāma-parāyaṇāḥ

apare niyatāhārāḥ prāṇān prāṇeṣhu juhvati

sarve 'pyete yajña-vido yajña-kṣhapita-kalmaṣhāḥ

31.

yajña-śhiṣhṭāmṛita-bhujo yānti brahma sanātanam

nāyaṁ loko 'styayajñasya kuto 'nyaḥ kuru-sattama

32.

evaṁ bahu-vidhā yajñā vitatā brahmaṇo mukhe

karma-jān viddhi tān sarvān evaṁ jñātvā vimokṣhyase

33.

śhreyān dravya-mayād yajñāj jñāna-yajñaḥ parantapa

sarvaṁ karmākhilaṁ pārtha jñāne parisamāpyate

34.

tad viddhi praṇipātena paripraśhnena sevayā

upadekṣhyanti te jñānaṁ jñāninas tattva-darśhinaḥ

35.

yaj jñātvā na punar moham evaṁ yāsyasi pāṇḍava

yena bhūtānyaśheṣheṇa drakṣhyasyātmanyatho mayi

36.

api ched asi pāpebhyaḥ sarvebhyaḥ pāpa-kṛit-tamaḥ

sarvaṁ jñāna-plavenaiva vṛijinaṁ santariṣhyasi

37.

yathaidhānsi samiddho 'gnir bhasma-sāt kurute 'rjuna

jñānāgniḥ sarva-karmāṇi bhasma-sāt kurute tathā

38.

na hi jñānena sadṛiśhaṁ pavitramiha vidyate

tatsvayaṁ yogasansiddhaḥ kālenātmani vindati

39.

śhraddhāvānllabhate jñānaṁ tat-paraḥ sanyatendriyaḥ

jñānaṁ labdhvā parāṁ śhāntim achireṇādhigachchhati

40.

ajñaśh chāśhraddadhānaśh cha sanśhayātmā vinaśhyati

nāyaṁ loko 'sti na paro na sukhaṁ sanśhayātmanaḥ

41.

yoga-sannyasta-karmāṇaṁ jñāna-sañchhinna-sanśhayam

ātmavantaṁ na karmāṇi nibadhnanti dhanañjaya

42.

tasmād ajñāna-sambhūtaṁ hṛit-sthaṁ jñānāsinātmanaḥ

chhittvainaṁ sanśhayaṁ yogam ātiṣhṭhottiṣhṭha bhārata

Contact

9839093003

myrichindia@gmail.com

facebook.com/drjagadeeshpillaiofficial

youtube.com/drjagadeeshpillai